Mourning Has Broken

Coming Out of the Dark

Marie Ceribelli

*Dedicated to all those who
struggle throughout life,
with a feeling of hopelessness.
It is never too late to make
changes in order to evolve
and become enlightened.
My hope is to inspire others
by sharing my story*

Knowing others is intelligence; knowing yourself is true wisdom. Mastering others is strength; mastering yourself is true power. If you realize that you have enough, you are truly rich.

(Lao Tzu, <u>Tao Te Ching)</u>

Table of Contents

PREFACE

The events that have occurred over my lifetime have led me to my current state of mind. Many tragic events have occurred, which has led to my self-examination. It will continue as long as I am still alive and breathing. I have found that I learn something new every day. The only difference now is that I no longer wait for tragedy to occur. I welcome change and I embrace all that is summoned to me – good or bad. I have had many turning points and awakenings before I was able to reach my inner peace and true happiness.

"As time goes marching by, but there's something wrong, we don't start living, until we almost die..."
("The Universe Listened" by Melissa Etheridge)

Introduction

What is personality? Personality is "who the person truly is and how she or he differs from other people. Particular biological tendencies and social cultural learning experiences combine to determine the person's uniqueness." (Ryckman, p. 23) Basically we become who we are because of all that happens to us. A person is like a puzzle – so many different pieces. "Just because we are influenced by our personality doesn't mean we have to be controlled by it." (Gary Chapman)

In the article, "You've Got Trauma, But Writing Can Help", written by Marilyn Elias, she states:

> Pouring your most painful traumas out on a computer screen can improve your health, according to one of the first studies on how e-mail may influence well-being. Evidence has

mounted in the past 15 years that writing in longhand about traumas- from rape to family deaths-leads to better mental and physical health. Now it looks as though laptop diaries or emails can work, too. (Elias)

I began writing several years ago and I have found it to be very therapeutic. My writing is done online. I have learned more about myself during this last decade of my life, than I did in my first forty years. It all began following the death of my father. His sudden and tragic death was my turning point. I began to read and write more than ever before. Three years later, I made the decision to enroll in college to educate myself. My husband was killed within two weeks of that decision. His death was my awakening and postponed my education for two years. It was soon after the death of my husband, that I began to speak publicly.

I was determined to become an educated human being!
I have been in school now for several years and I am
working towards my Bachelor's degree. I am amazed at all I
have learned and continue to learn. I realize that I have been
an angry and bitter person for most of my life, but I no
longer allow my pain or anger to control my life. I have
learned to take ownership of my pain and anger and I control
it. It's okay to feel sad and cry from time to time, as long as
one does not dwell for too long. I have learned to embrace
my pain and anger, as it is a part of me and who I am. Pain
and suffering have led to my enlightenment, therefore I am
grateful. It has been quite a journey and it continues.

Gratitude unlocks the fullness of life. It turns what we have into enough, and more. It turns denial into acceptance, chaos to order, confusion to clarity. It can turn a meal into a feast, a house into a home, a stranger into a friend. Gratitude makes sense of our past, brings peace for today, and creates a vision for tomorrow. (Melody Beattie)

Demographic Background

I am the daughter of an Irish-American mother and an Arab-American father. Both parents were born in Brooklyn, New York. My mother also had English, French and German descendants, but she related mostly to her Irish side. My maternal grandparents were born in New York and my paternal grandparents emigrated from Syria when they were young. None of my grandparents had an easy, happy life. My mother's parents, who had three children, suffered from various hardships, her mother suffered from polio and her father struggled with alcoholism. My father's parents, who had four children, also had a hard life. His father suffered from diabetes, which claimed his life when he was only sixty-three years old and his mother suffered the loss of her two sons, who were both in their forties.

My parents met in high school and married when they were twenty years old. After the birth of my brother, my mother suffered three miscarriages before she had me six years after my brother's birth. Four years later she gave birth to identical twin boys, and at the age of forty, she gave birth to another boy who lived for only two days. Looking at old photographs it seemed that my parents were very much in love when they first married, but after suffering through the miscarriages and then losing their baby so soon after his birth, it all put a strain on their marriage. I would have had two more brothers and two sisters had they all survived. My parents cared and provided for my brothers and I, but they were only "good enough" parents, they could have been better or they could have been worse. They were young and uneducated parents, as was I.

What they lacked in parenting they more than made up for when they became grandparents. My dad taught his grandchildren how to fish and he shared his love of the ocean with them. He also taught them how to shoot pool, play chess and he really enjoyed interacting with them every chance he could. My dad was an amazing chef and taught me how to cook. He shared his love for food with his children and grandchildren. My mother was also very involved with her grandchildren, especially when they were younger because she had their full and undivided attention. Her favorite holidays were Halloween and Valentine's Day, and she made an event out of both of them, particularly Valentine's Day which she called "Love Day."

My dad had a massive heart attack and died suddenly and unexpectantly at the age of sixty-nine years old. My mom suffered from dementia and passed away at seventy-nine years old. Their deaths were ten years apart to the day.

I was married when I was twenty years old and had my first child when I was twenty-four years of age. I now have three adult children. I became widowed several years ago and have since remarried. My second marriage has given me stepchildren and my oldest daughter and son-in-law have blest me with my first grandchild. My children are now young adults, which allows me plenty of time for myself. It has been a long and winding road. Here is my story.

Early Life

I was born in Park Slope, Brooklyn, New York.

Prospect Park was my backyard. It was and still is a great

neighborhood. When I look back at pictures of myself when

I was a very young child, I appear to look so sad. It was

not until recently that I figured out why. A few years back, I

learned that if an expectant mother has emotional pain or

fear, it can be transferred to her unborn child. That newborn

baby can be born angry. My mother had suffered three

miscarriages before I was born. My mother feared another

miscarriage. It does make sense, as my parents were thrilled

to have had me, as I was considered the "miracle baby".

When I was four years old, my younger twin brothers were

born. My mother seemed to be extremely tired and stressed

as the twins were a lot to handle. My mom and I did not

have a close relationship, I was closer to my dad. I maintained the status of "daddy's little girl" forever. Perhaps it was because I felt as if my mom was absent, as she was so busy with the twins and I idolized my dad more. She slept a lot during that time, when she could. During my adolescence, my mom seemed more depressed and was always sleeping to avoid her unhappy marital state. When I was twelve years old, my mother had another baby boy. He was born prematurely and died after two days. She was forty years old at the time. We had hoped that the new baby would bring our parents back together. I grew up surrounded by family. My cousins and I grew up together and still remain very close. I have a wonderful family! It is a large crowd. My family and I celebrate many holidays, birthdays and barbeques together. When I look back at the home movies, everyone was eating, drinking, smoking, and dancing…celebrating life and love. No apartment was ever too small for us all. Life was simple.

I grew up in a Catholic household. My brothers and I went to Catholic schools from first grade through high school. We were disciplined at home and at school. I think it was a good thing. My brothers and I were always respectful towards others. Having my cousins around all of the time was like having an extended family. My female cousins became sisters to me. My aunts are mentors to me.

When I was five years old my family and I moved to another neighborhood in Kensington, Brooklyn, New York. It was a beautiful house with a large backyard and a swimming pool, which was rare in Brooklyn, as the backyards are usually very small. I grew up in a very close-knit neighborhood. Everybody knew each other, therefore you did not fear venturing off your block. I still have a relationship with my neighbors of yesteryear.

Growing up in Brooklyn has made me street-wise. Having

lived in three different boroughs, I have found the

Brooklynites to be the warmest of people. I cherish the

summer nights when we all just sat outside on our stoops. I

could not have asked for a better place to have grown-up.

During my grammar school years, I was very shy and

timid. I kept to myself most of the time. I had two good

friends on my block, one girl and one boy, they were all that

I needed. I became more social during my high school years.

When I met my first husband and high school sweetheart, I

then began to blossom.

Positive Influences

My family and my neighborhood jointly had a positive influence on the person I have become. The times shared with family and friends are cherished times, life's treasures to me. Through all the craziness life has to offer, we always manage to pull together. I have learned and continue to learn so much from all that has happened – good, bad and indifferent. My father taught me to be strong and my mother taught me to be independent. I have learned to rely only on myself and not to depend on anyone else. My first husband and I shared our love for old traditions and morals.

Through my work with M.A.D.D., I have met with many wonderful psychologists and speakers. I trained to become a victim advocate to learn even more and to also help and support other victims. I found speaking to be very therapeutic and fulfilling. It is a wonderful feeling to be able to give something back and to realize that you may be helping another person. When I speak of my late husband, I fall in love with him all over again. I have forgotten most of the bad stuff we have been through and I remind myself of all his good qualities. I describe to the audience the life that was taken away before I explain the aftermath and devastation drunk driving has caused for my family and I, from the moment he was killed to the present time.

My current education has been an extremely positive influence in my life. I have met the most amazing professors and classmates. The courses I have studied have helped me to realize so much more than I ever could have imagined.

I had one philosophy professor who became more of a therapist and mentor to me. I took several classes with him. Some of the stories and plays that I have read in my English classes mirrored my life. It was astounding! My professors and my son have encouraged me to write my story and to share it with others.

I had attended a lecture on campus given by Elie Wiesel and found him to be very inspirational. As I listened to Mr. Wiesel speak, I could not help but to reflect on my own personal life experiences. He spoke of repairing the world, humanity and our souls. He spoke of the effect of death and survival. He also spoke of morality, loyalty and indifference. Elie also spoke of the art of survival. He spoke of what was necessary in order to survive – such as generosity, hope, solidarity and the passion for learning. He seemed humble and sincere, as life has had the same effect on my own well-being. Elie had mentioned how the unthinkable can happen and the impossible can become possible. I knew that all too well.

All my children and grandchild are positive influences in my life, as when I see the goodness in them, I feel accomplished. They give me hope for the future and yet they remind me of the past. I cherish our special moments together. They warm my heart and when life gets too difficult they are my anchors and my reason to carry on.

My current husband has been a positive influence in my life. We have the same outlook on life now. Prior to meeting him, we have both had our share of troubles in past years. Now we spend each day just being kind and loving towards one another. We have learned to embrace the past, as it will always be a part of us. We enjoy each and every day together. We constantly laugh and I do believe it is the best medicine. He is extremely supportive of my work with M.A.D.D. He is great with my children and he lives with the ghost of my late husband. He accepts my family and my first in-law family as his own family now. I could not think of a better person to grow old with. He has an amazing sense of humor, which will be needed as we grow older.

I have attended so many concerts during this period of mourning and grief, that I believe it was to remind me of happier times and to feel happiness instead of sadness. I cannot imagine my life without music! Seeing certain artists felt like I was visiting with old friends. Music takes me to places of yesteryear and reminds me of those who I have lost...in a happy way. It also takes me to places I have never been. Music has a calming effect on me as well.

New songs are symbolic of my new relationships and new beginnings. I love singing a tune! Without music I would feel dead inside. Singing and dancing is what my mother instilled in me. She sang and danced every chance she could, as it made her feel alive. Singing has that same effect on me, however I am not much of a dancer...yet. I will forever be grateful to her for that. The following song became my anthem:

Lessons Learned
by Carrie Underwood

There's some things that I regret,
Some words I wish had gone unsaid,
Some starts,
That had some bitter endings,

Been some bad times I've been through,

Damage I cannot undo,

Some things,

I wish I could do all over again,

But it don't really matter,

Life gets that much harder,

It makes you that much stronger,

Oh, some pages turned,

Some bridges burned,

But there were,

Lessons learned.

[Chorus:]

And every tear that had to fall from my eyes,

Everyday I wondered how I'd get through the night,

Every change, life has thrown me,

I'm thankful, for every break in my heart,

I'm grateful, for every scar,

Some pages turned,

Some bridges burned,

But there were lessons learned.

There's mistakes that I have made,

Some chances I just threw away,

Some roads,

I never should've taken,

Been some signs I didn't see,

Hearts that I hurt needlessly,

Some wounds,

That I wish I could have one more chance to mend,

But it don't make no difference,

The past can't be rewritten,

You get the life you're given,

Oh, some pages turned,

Some bridges burned,

But there were,

Lessons learned.

[Chorus:]

And every tear that had to fall from my eyes,

Everyday I wondered how I'd get through the night,

Every change, life has thrown me,

I'm thankful, for every break in my heart,

I'm grateful, for every scar,

Some pages turned,

Some bridges burned,

But there were lessons learned.

And all the things that break you,

Are all the things that make you strong,

You can't change the past,

Cause it's gone,

And you just gotta move on,

Because it's all,

Lessons learned.

[Chorus:]

And every tear that had to fall from my eyes,

Everyday I wondered how I'd get through the night,

Every change, life has thrown me,

I'm thankful, for every break in my heart,

I'm grateful, for every scar,

Some pages turned,

Some bridges burned,

But there were lessons learned,

Oh, some pages turned,

Some bridges burned,

But there were lessons learned,

Lessons learned.

I truly love that song, it is so very true. Songs are like poems or sonnets and at times can be very philosophical and inspirational. Messages are sent through music, making music very therapeutic.

Music gives a soul to the universe,

wings to the mind, flight to the

imagination and life to everything.

(Plato)

Problems

I cannot remember a time in my life when there were no problems. They are lessons in life and I believe problems are a crucial part of life. When I was a young child I was inappropriately touched. This happened a few times before I had the courage to tell my mother. It was never spoken about and dropped after that. For many years that followed, I was unable to trust and allow myself to be touched. My coping strategy was to build internal walls within myself. That incident stole many years of my life.

Years later, when I was a teenager, my parents' marriage began to crumble and unravel. They lived their separate lives, under the same roof. My dad was a gambler and in his later years he became an alcoholic. My mother suffered from depression and was verbally and sometimes

physically abused by my father. This depression led my
mother to sleep through my teenage years. I became a
mother figure to my younger brothers. There were a few
times when my mother left us. The only way I could contact
her was at her workplace. I had become resentful during that
time because I had a household to manage and children to
care for at the young age of twelve. My parents finally
divorced after thirty-seven years of marriage. My father lost
his restaurant due to his bad habits and addictions. After
their divorce, they went their separate ways. Both my
parents never openly brought another person into their or our
lives.

When I was twenty years old I married my first
husband. My husband and I grew up together and planned
on growing old together. Life was simple and easy in the

beginning, until he became self-employed. He was a carpenter and a contractor by trade. Work was not always steady, leaving us with a great deal of financial stress. Our parents were always there to help us out to the point where it became enabling and crippling. Our financial difficulties caused so much tension in our once happy home. He became verbally abusive to me and I became a compulsive overeater as a result. Food was my comfort. He displaced his frustration onto me and I displaced my anger onto my children. It was a horrible time which lasted for approximately ten years. I did not like the unhappy environment we had created for our family.

During that time, my father-in-law passed away after suffering from congestive heart failure for thirteen years. It was thirteen years of near-death experiences for him.

He was like a walking time-bomb. He passed away one day before we were to move into a new house, in a new borough. Our move was postponed two weeks because of his death. We moved from Staten Island to Queens to be closer to my husband's place of business, as he was tired of the daily commute and getting home late. My husband loved his children and wanted to spend more time with them. Our plan backfired, as we were in a new place and neither one of us was working. During that time, we were all depressed over the loss of my father-in-law, making it that much harder to get back on track again.

Moving to Queens put me closer to my father, and he visited us once or twice a week. He filled the void that my family and I were experiencing due to the loss of my father-in-law. Unfortunately, it was short-lived. Less than two years after my father-in-law's death, my father died. My father was in a heated argument with my husband at the time of his death. My father suffered a massive heart attack in front of my children and I. It was horrifying to stand by and watch. That night was the worst night of my life, but yet one can say it may have been the best night of my life, as it has changed me drastically. I felt so alone and helpless as I watched my father take his last breath. He died in my home. My father's death brought many childhood issues to the surface. I felt so much rage and anger during that time.

Three years after my father's death, my husband was killed by a drunk driver. My family and I were beyond devastated. He was a healthy forty-four year old man. His death really stunned so many people. There was so much anger and outrage. I was destroyed emotionally, physically

and financially. I felt as if I was at the bottom of a deep dark
well with no way out. It was a very dark and lonely place to
be. I was medicated for two years to help me cope and
survive. I was very vulnerable during that time. I wallowed
in self-pity and decided that it did not pay to be good, so I
went out and behaved very badly. I became promiscuous
and forgot all the morals and values I once knew. The
passion I felt was so intense because of the grief and pain I
was feeling. I still cannot believe all that I had done during
that time. As a result of my husband's untimely death, my
two youngest children and myself acted out with self-
destructive behaviors. The three main men in our lives were
all dead within five years.

The drunk driver who killed my husband was
arrested and released on bail. He was caught driving drunk

again one month after killing my husband, he had a gun in his van the second time. He was arrested again and held without bail until his sentencing. He went to prison for two years. He served one year for killing my husband and one year for the gun charge. I had filed a criminal lawsuit, followed by a civil lawsuit. Six years of my life was spent running to several different attorneys. I had to constantly take time off from work for one thing or another pertaining to the lawsuits. I also had to clear my every move with my attorney beforehand. I had to keep reliving what had happened and deal with all of its' unpleasantries. Several years later, my children and I met with the drunk driver to help with our healing process. I hope that someday they realize the importance of that meeting.

I came to realize that most of my life I have been surrounded by alcoholism. My dad was an alcoholic.

I do not recall him drinking when I was a young child, however, I do remember him drinking in his later years. I can remember laughing with my brothers about how he would park his car on the driveway on a night when he had been drinking. I cannot imagine my children laughing at such a thing today. My dad had left my engagement party early because of his drunken state and he drove himself home. My uncle, too, was an alcoholic and died at the age of forty-three years old. I was thirteen years old at the time. I remember the smell of his bedroom and all the empty bottles in his garbage pail. I do not think he ever left his bedroom. He became a recluse from what I can remember. My maternal grandfather was a "weekend alcoholic" as my mom would call him. I never knew there was such a thing. I seem to come from a family of addictive personalities. I have seen family members and close friends suffer from alcoholism. Some of whom have succumbed, while others have recovered and continue to live their lives in sobriety. My hope is that this fate never falls on to my children. My children have endured so much in their young lives and the pain and anger can be intense at times. What the younger generation does not understand is that alcoholism is a very slow progression. People usually do not realize they have a problem until they are much older. Alcoholism is devastating to all those involved – the alcoholics and their family members and friends. It is difficult to watch those you love struggle. My cousin-in-law was killed by a drunk driver when he was seventeen years old.

Cancer is another disease that has taken many family members. My father's brother died from colon cancer when he was forty-six years old, leaving my father with no living brothers. My maternal grandmother died from cervical cancer. My cousin died at fifty-two years old from breast cancer. I lost another cousin to liver cancer. I lost three aunts, two to lung cancer and one to stomach cancer. I have cousins who have survived cancer and are still here today. My nephew beat leukemia and is now in remission.

The idea of overcoming is always fascinating to me. It's fascinating because few of us realize how much energy we have expended just to be here today. I don't think we give ourselves enough credit for the overcoming. (Maya Angelou)

It takes so much time, energy and work in order to be able to overcome something. Most people do not understand and others are not willing to do what it takes in order to become well or better. It is an extremely difficult journey and long process.

Accept — then act. Whatever the present moment contains, accept it as if you had chosen it. Always work with it, not against it. Make it your friend and ally, not your enemy. This will miraculously transform your whole life. (Eckhart Tolle)

Education and All I Have Learned

I never realized how uneducated I was until I enrolled in college at the age of forty-six years old. It saddened me to learn the damage my parents have done to me, and I to my children, all because we were all so uneducated. As I continue to learn, I share all that I have learned with my adult children. I try to undo the damage I have caused. They laugh at me and reassure me that they are fine. My son always tells me he had the best childhood. It was not always so bad and I know we cannot go back in time, only forward. I have since apologized for my past behavior and I have let go of all feelings of guilt and resentment.

My first two classes in college were English I and English II. I enrolled in one class per semester, because I felt I should take it slow, I also thought there would be a lot of writing involved. In my very first class, the professor asked the class to write down what we thought a hero was and then what a tragic hero was. I wrote that my late husband was a tragic hero, as I felt he died while he was working to provide for his family. I had no clue where the professor was going with this. During the semester we read plays and novels, and in each play, we had to state how the main character of each story was a tragic hero. It turns out that the tragic hero of each story died. All of those characters had the same flaws and characteristics of my late husband. It was mind-boggling!

I also took several philosophy classes. One class was on the seven deadly sins and I learned so much about myself and those closest to me. I met a naturopedic doctor who explained how a baby can be born with anger. I never even considered the thought, until it was mentioned. It was like a

light bulb went on inside my head, an epiphany! As a very

young child, I never really appeared to be happy. I rarely

smiled or laughed and always looked so sad. I knew

my parents were thrilled to have had me and referred to me

as their "miracle baby". This doctor explained how fear and

pain lead to anger and that anger can be transferred from the

mother to her unborn baby through the amniotic fluid. If an

expectant mother is anxious or angry, the water molecules

will change. My mom had the fear of possibly having

another miscarriage. I was not looking to place blame and as

I mentioned earlier, I had never given it any thought.

Unexpectantly, that thought came to me that night in class.

It was a great feeling as I was still continuing to learn about myself! Then, I thought of my own pregnancy with my youngest daughter. I witnessed two sudden deaths during that pregnancy; my childhood friend who was killed in a car accident and my aunt who died from a brain aneurysm. I remember feeling very upset and concerned for the well-being of my unborn child. The doctor reassured me that she would be fine. My youngest daughter seems angry some of the time for no apparent reason and now I see that this may have started even before her birth.

The anger I had had since my childhood began to dissipate as I learned how to forgive, even the unforgiveable. "An open mind and a forgiving spirit can pave the way for you to objectively view your past." (Gary Chapman) In one of my philosophy classes, I learned that anger is an addiction that a person can change with the proper help and guidance. Anger can lead to enlightenment. Anger is a cognitive addiction and if one could let go of anger, he or she could become superior and rise above. People need to get rid of the poisons. Life is suffering, there will always be pain or loss, sooner or later. Patience and tolerance are needed to be free of anger. To shift awareness, one must shift their consciousness. For the most part, people get angry at other things and take the anger out on someone else, for no apparent reason. Sometimes people see what they are lacking in others and that makes them angry. Anger has an energy of its' own, but it can be changed into something positive. It is all about awareness and recognizing the fact that you are angry. Eroding the absolute self is central. One must begin with a beginner's mind and start from scratch. I also believe that anger can be a learned behavior as well. I think that anger, for the most part, is the core or underlying reason for all the deadly sins. I now choose to live my life without remaining angry. I have learned how to switch my thoughts to happier and more pleasant thoughts when I do become angry at times. I also breathe and meditate now to help myself relax. When one becomes enlightened, he or she then becomes passive. One who is passive is much more relaxed and healthier than one who is aggressive and tense. Anger led me to my enlightenment, therefore I am grateful.

Lust has a mental companion, as does love. The two can be very misunderstood. I believe that lust has two faces and I have seen lust from both sides – bliss and woe. In my personal experience, pain, fear and anger had led to my lustful behavior and promiscuity, leaving me with a feeling of emptiness. It is more fulfilling to be in a relationship where there is a lustful love, combatibility and no inhibitions. It is not an easy thing to come by, it took me forty-five years to find that kind of love.

As for greed, the more conflicted life becomes, the more susceptible one can become to greed. The more one craves or desires, the more greedy one becomes. I think greed is a combination of sins, resulting in greediness. The definition of greed in and of itself can read: intense longing (lust), especially for food or wealth (gluttony), desire (avarice) and craving. I have learned to appreciate what I have and not want more than what I need in order to survive.

Envy is always secretive, as it is not a good feeling. There can be some confusion between envy and jealousy. People are ashamed of being envious and people who are envious tend to act or appear phony to those who do not know them well enough. They can say one thing, but really mean something else. Envy can turn into malice and envious people have the tendency to wish bad will onto others. Negative prehension and resentment go hand-in-hand with envy. Resentment is more passive than envy. Resentment is a self-poisoning of the mind. It is a lasting mental attitude. Maybe at certain times in one's life, one can tend to be envious. For example: when someone is down or depressed, he or she may become envious of someone else's life. The grass always seems greener on the other side, for some people. Gratitude is essential to becoming truly happy. If one is grateful, he or she then would have no reason to become envious.

Gluttony has evolved along with our ideas about salvation and damnation, health and illness, life and death. Today gluttony has transformed from a sin into an illness and has become clinicalized. Today, gluttony is the fact that one overeats out of compulsion and is self-destructive to avoid intimacy and social contact. But gluttony is also a pleasure. Gluttony is the most visible of the deadly sins. Unlike envy, one cannot hide gluttony. I believe that gluttony is the most obvious and the easiest to be perceived by the untutored eye. There is definitely a connection to overeating and a person's mental health. Some people eat for comfort. People put food into their bodies instead of their minds. At times one may become a glutton, but gluttony is not just one occasional event, it is a condition. When I received the news that my mom was placed in a nursing home, I found myself looking for something to eat, but I was not hungry. I was looking to food for comfort. The difference during that time was that I was aware of my behavior and I stopped myself from eating. It is all about thinking and controlling thoughts. I am an emotional eater. I am still learning about my own addictive behaviors. I now have heart disease because of my old habits and addictions. I no longer overeat, but the damage is done. However, I can change the behavior and improve my health, as it is never too late.

Lust, Greed, Anger, Envy and Gluttony are definitely deadly sins. Deadly, not necessarily in just the physical sense. These sins can cause death in a spiritual way as well as in a physical way. They could also cause the death of any relationship, between parents and their children, siblings, friends and significant others. I believe that at some point these sins can all be intertwined with one another. I feel that anger is the main core or cause of most of these deadly sins. Anger stole many years of my life and led me to lust and gluttony. I believe that pride and envy led my late husband to his untimely death. He would constantly say, "Why me?" and he was quick to place blame. He felt a sense of entitlement as well. He was too proud to become an employee once again, especially after being self-employed for so many years. He also became very resentful during those extremely difficult times. It was not until three weeks prior to his death, that he finally began working for a general contractor, as an employee, but he was still able to act like a boss. He was allowed to run the jobs and hire his own workers with no questions asked. It was his dream come true and he was just too happy! He died on that construction site three weeks after starting that job. After all that I have learned, I now feel compassion for him, as he had become so frustrated and desperate towards the end of his life. I, in turn became resentful when I became a widow, as I did not appreciate being left behind to deal with three grieving teenagers. I did not want the daunting task that lied ahead. I am truly grateful these deadly sins have not taken my life. I am extremely fortunate for my new found awareness and second chance at living life well.

My other philosophy class was about the great founders of philosophy- Plato, Socrates, Descartes and Mill. I really enjoyed Plato's' book, The Republic, as there is a section in the book entitled "The Allegory of the Cave". The people inside the cave live in darkness. Those who escape from the cave become enlightened while those people left behind are thought to be ignorant. It is believed by Plato that as one leaves the cave, he or she is led into the lightness. Metaphorically, the people inside the cave are us. If one is freed and let out of the cave, that person would be blinded by the light and suffer pain and distress. At first, the person would still see shadows and think that they are real. As the person is dragged out of the cave, he or she will be in great pain and resent being taken outside into the sunlight until he or she grows accustomed to it. As one adjusts to real life objects and reality, he or she will then be able to see clearly. It is just like life itself, as the experience of being dragged out of the cave can be compared to certain experiences in one's life. When a baby is first born he or she can only see shadows but as the child grows into an adult, his or her life experiences can lead him or her towards the light. People learn from life experiences. Inside the cave there is little or no knowledge – only darkness and ignorance. Unfortunately, this is how most people spend most of their lives – close-minded, not knowing. Outside the cave is the road to truth, knowledge and reality – enlightenment. If a person were to re-enter the cave and try to share what he or she has learned, the people inside the cave would look at him or her as if he or she were crazy. They would refuse to believe or listen to the enlightened person. One's personal experience or knowledge differs from someone else's. Some people need to be dragged by some other force, while others need a teacher or some form of guidance to help lead them to the truth.

All people have the possibility to be brought to greater knowledge. It is usually a turn of events that can cause people to search for the truth. Confusion inspires thinking and is the mother of enlightenment. Truth is better than deception and falsehood. Socrates believes that it is worth "being" just for its own sake. He compares a city to a person and how all sectors need to be operating properly in order for a city or a person to become "just" or work properly and sufficiently. He spoke of three virtues: temperance, courage, and wisdom. Within a person there are the body (temperance), the spirit (courage), and the mind (wisdom). Temperance impacts a person as he or she needs to have willpower in order to control his or her appetite and desire. As for courage, this is necessary for a person's emotional needs in order to be able to reason and think properly. And lastly wisdom, which I personally believe comes with aging. People learn from their mistakes or should I say lessons in life. It is never too late in life to learn and make changes. If there is temperance and courage, then a person will be able to reason more clearly. If a "just" person is temperant in his or her desires and lives courageously; he or she then reasons to make better choices. However, it is not always that simple. Certain life situations can cause a person to become "unjust." From my own personal experience, I have found certain times in my life when I had become unjust and therefore unreasonable.

I took another philosophy class on the interpretation of dreams. It taught me that all those events that had occurred during the course of a lifetime are all banked in the subconscious mind. The subconscious mind is like a mother board on a computer, it is all saved there. Prior to taking this course, I was in a good place mentally and recovering from all that had taken place prior in my life. I had made peace with it all...or so I thought. I had to keep a dream journal and record the dreams that I was able to remember. It was amazing to analyze my dreams, as they were not always what they appeared to be. Sometimes dreams are just what they seem to be. I became anxious in knowing what my dreams meant, as I thought I was passed all that had happened and was over it. Some things can never be over. I had come to realize that some things come to the surface when we are dreaming, especially if they were traumatic events. Sometimes your thoughts can be triggered and come to fruition in your dreams. One must learn how to cope and react when certain memories resurface. All in all, it was quite interesting to say the very least. This was yet another learning experience for me.

The Tao te Ching has become my favorite book, the central philosophical ideas contained in the Tao te Ching are the virtues of compassion, patience, simplicity and peace. In verse 69, Lao Tzu speaks of compassion when he says, "victory will go to those who take no delight in the situation." He is stating that one should not rush to judgment and should take a step back to take a better look. One should yield and be more rational towards others. The treasure he speaks of is peace of mind. To live in an "enemy-less" land. In verse 36, Lao Tzu speaks of patience and simplicity, "If you want to shrink something, you have to allow it to expand." He is basically stating that soft overcomes hard, but one must be patient and live slowly. It is a long process in order to expand or grow and then to realize that less is more in order to get back to the simple things in life. Lao Tzu believes that one should live with the wisdom of obscurity in order to eliminate competition. One should stay in the background and not draw attention. One should not compare themself to others. One should learn to substitute "I" for "you". Lao Tzu speaks of peace in verse 16, when he says, "Become totally empty. Let your heart be at peace." In this verse he explains how one should stay in the present moment and not become distracted. One should keep an empty and a "big blue sky" mind. Lao Tzu suggests that one should live with constancy, as change is constant. One must accept change and alter ego-based thoughts in order to be in harmony. When you change how you look at things, things will change. One must learn how to return to the source where all cycles begin and end. One needs to stay aware. My favorite quote is, "Muddy water, let stand – becomes clear", meaning where there is turmoil or confusion, eventually you will be able to see clearly. I have read the <u>Tao te Ching</u> several times, and it is how I live my life now.

Meditation has been something I have found to be necessary in order to remain calm and at peace. It is also needed to remain healthy and less anxious. It does not matter for how long one meditates, but it is something that should be done on a daily basis, especially before going to sleep at night. Meditation is a time for relaxing and clearing one's mind of all thoughts. Philosophy has taught me how to switch my thoughts to better ones. It has also taught me the art of meditation. I wish I could help others master the art of meditation as it feels so wonderful afterwards.

After my heart disease diagnosis, I had decided to enroll into a nutrition class. I thought it would be beneficial for all my ailments and diseases. The word disease is interesting to me as it could mean dis-ease, not at ease with one's self - philosophically or psychologically, as mental health leads to physical health. I currently have asthma, hypothyroidism and heart disease. It was so interesting to me to learn exactly how and why disease is caused. Basically it is because of what our bodies ingest, such as food, beverages and the air that we breathe. I was surprised to learn that heredity plays a small role in disease and that one can change and improve one's health. There went my excuse. My professor explained that to eat properly, one must ingest all five food groups at every meal and one must also practice portion control and eat in moderation. She also stated that there are no bad foods and that we can get all our nutrients from the food that we eat. Variety in the foods that are eaten is also of major importance. One must also learn how to read food labels as they can be misleading. I became the poster-person for heart disease in that class and I shared my experience with my younger classmates. I have since made some lifestyle changes. I make better food choices and I also keep a daily journal of all that I consume, however I struggle with variety and portion control. I do cardiovascular exercise first thing every morning. It is a very slow process as I had to become mentally well first. In my first forty years, I had single-handedly done so much damage to myself. It is now time to undo that damage, since it's never too late. I no longer get stressed over my weight, I just do and be the best I can be every day. I am aware of my behavior, which is difficult to stop or change after so many years. Behavior is the main cause and problem of all bad habits and addictions. I had come to the realization that I was once an over-compulsive eater. I approach this one day at a time, food is a substance like alcohol and drugs and can become addicting. Awareness is the first step, followed by taking action and making changes. My blood work has never been better. This will continue to be a work in progress, and my goal is to one day decrease my medication dosages.

After taking my psychopharmacology and substance abuse classes, I became horrified as I learned about tobacco, alcohol and drugs in more depth. The damage that is caused is known by so many, yet so many people continue to struggle to give up their bad and unhealthy habits. I now understand more about the addiction gene, which is inherently on both sides of my family. Those who abuse any substance, are simply self-medicating themselves from the fear, pain and anger that lies within. Life can become difficult and extremely unbearable at times.

In my forensic psychology, neuroscience and differential diagnosis classes, I learned so much about the brain and how it works. I learned about all the hormones and chemicals in our bodies that at times make us behave strangely and why and how criminals become serial killers. I have also learned that I should not use the word crazy too often, as there is usually something causing the strange or odd behavior. I now know how to diagnose and really observe people. These three classes were extremely informative and interesting. In my abnormal psychology and personality classes I learned that people are complex beings. There are so many things that contribute to who and what a person turns out to be such as heredity, birth order, learned behavior and situational circumstances, hence why siblings tend to be different from one another.

As my second wedding was approaching, I decided to take a sociology class on families, as my family was now to become a blended family. I never actually knew the true definition of marriage until I took this class. That may sound strange, as I was married for twenty-four years before I became widowed.

> Marriage is a social union or legal contract between people called spouses that establishes rights and obligations between the spouses, between the spouses and their children, and between the spouses and their in-laws. The definition of marriage varies according to different cultures, but it is principally an institution in which interpersonal

relationships, usually intimate and sexual, are

acknowledged. (Wikipedia)

I was only twenty years old when I married the first

time. My husband and I were both so very young, innocent

and uneducated. Marriage for us was the next step after

dating each other for a few years. We were in love and

wanted to start a family, and it was also the only way to

move out of our parents' home. Marriage at fifty-three years

old is totally different than at twenty years old. Marriage is a

social contract and commitment, it's about certain benefits as

we grow older. My second husband and I accept each other

for who we are and who we have become and do not plan on

changing for one another. At fifty–three years old we have

both grown more patient and tolerant.

Honest concern for others is the key factor in

improving our day to day lives. When you are

warmhearted, there is no room for anger,
jealousy or insecurity. A calm mind and
self-confidence are the basis for happy and
peaceful relations with each other. Happy,
happy families and a healthy peaceful nation
are dependent on warmheartedness.
(Dalai Lama)

We have raised our children, and have learned not to let our adult children offend us or interfere in our relationship – no matter what they may say or do. We are each other's equal and we respect one another. Whereas, in my first marriage, because we were so young, one of us evolved and the other one did not. My husband and I have learned that acts of kindness go a very long way. We love and laugh daily. We are still role models for our children, no matter how old they may be. We put time aside for ourselves, together as a couple and individually as well. We do not smother one another and we do not make any demands on our children.

I also took a sociology class on human sexuality to better understand all that is going on in today's society. I wish I had taken this class several years ago when I had become widowed and when my children were teenagers. Through my sociology and psychology classes I came to realize that the incident that had occurred when I was a young child was definitely a wrongful act and my confusion was legit. In regards to sex, there is so much to know about in today's society, such as to why people behave in a certain manner. The chapter on human trafficking was frightening to me as it still happens often and in nearby areas. The pornography industry is a constant growing industry world-wide. I learned about prostitution and legal brothels. I also learned some terminology, such as "hooking up" and how it has several different meanings. I learned the differences between homosexual, bisexual, bicurious and transgender. Some of what I had learned was very confusing to me, however I found it to be very fascinating.

As I began my last year of school, I took my last two required classes – "Experimental Psychology II" and the "History of Modern Philosophy". Experimental psychology taught me about learning and conditioning. I think I learned as much from my lab rat as he learned from me. I wish I had known more about positive reinforcement when my children were younger. I cannot wait to use what I have learned on my grandson. In modern day philosophy, many of the philosophers were scientists first. Those scientists who were mentioned in my experimental psychology class, were Locke, Galileo and Descartes, they were also philosophers.

It was all very interesting as the modern day philosophers' ideas and ideals were geared more towards science and nature, instead of religion, which were very different from the ancient philosophers' views that Aristotle, Plato and Socrates had. I also had the opportunity to read works written by Kant and Emerson. I especially enjoyed Emerson's works, he states, "What lies behind us, and what lies before us are but tiny matters compared to what lies within us...Make the most of yourself, for that is all there is of you." I found Ralph Waldo Emerson to be very inspirational. He too, had suffered great loss and pain. I found his life story to be so interesting.

Also in my senior year, I had found a music class on the Beatles. What a way to end my year! I thoroughly enjoyed this class and all that I have learned. Some material I had already known and some material was new to me.

My entire life has been surrounded by the Beatles and their music. My late husband was an avid Beatles' fan. The Beatles were a huge part of our relationship and now my family and I remember my late husband through their music. As my senior year came to a close, I could not help but reflect on all the people in my life past and present who have helped me along this journey. Some have touched me in ways they could never understand or imagine. A song that comes to mind is, "In My Life" by the Beatles that reflects all the mixed emotions that I felt as I completed my Bachelor's degree.

In My Life
by The Beatles

There are places I remember

All my life, though some have changed

Some forever not for better

Some have gone and some remain

All these places had their moments

With lovers and friends

I still can recall

Some are dead and some are living

In my life I've loved them all

But of all these friends and lovers

There is no one compares with you

And these memories lose their meaning

When I think of love as something new

Though I know I'll never lose affection

For people and things that went before

I know I'll often stop and think about them

In my life I love you more

Post-Traumatic Stress

I had started my research on Post-Traumatic Stress, a year after my late husband was tragically and suddenly killed by a drunk driver. I needed to know what this was and how to cope and deal with what had happened to my family and I. What amazes me is the fact that I believe I have suffered from post-traumatic stress for most of my life, going as far back as my early childhood. My education has enhanced what I have learned about myself and has taught me how to better deal with my family who continues to suffer from time to time.

Post-traumatic stress is not necessarily caused by just one tragic event in one's life, it can also be caused by a long term stressor. It can consume you and I was not aware of that until my research began. "Post-traumatic Stress

Disorder (PTSD): Symptoms, Types and Treatment" is an article I had come across online. Post-Traumatic Stress Disorder seems to be a combination of many different emotions and behaviors. Before researching this topic, I thought post-traumatic stress was something that was caused by one specific tragic or traumatic event that happened to one person. I have learned that post-traumatic stress can be caused by long term abuse or stress of any kind. There are physiological, psychological and social outcomes. Post-traumatic stress can also lead to self-destructive behaviors.

When I was a young child I was inappropriately touched, as mentioned earlier. I was paid not to tell anyone, I felt my violator knew he was performing a wrongful act, as I was paid to keep quiet. This happened a few times before I finally had the courage to tell my mother. It was never spoken about again. I held that inside me for most of my life and I kept it a secret. I did not confront that person until many decades later. He refused to believe that he did anything wrong and claimed it was an act of curiosity, and perhaps in his mindset it was, but it was very disturbing for me at that young age. I was a young child and I did not know anything about sex. I came to the conclusion that he was more curious about the mechanics of the act itself and not just the typical physical differences between girls and boys. It has taken many years for me to accept the fact that maybe it was just curiosity on his part, and he really had no intention of hurting me. It took many years into my adulthood to realize that and overcome it. As I had continued to read and learn, I had read a few books written by Eckhart Tolle. One of his quotes that comes to mind is:

Life will give you whatever experience is
helpful for the evolution of your

consciousness. How do you know this is the
experience you need? Because this is the
experience you are having at this moment.
(Eckhart Tolle)

I now know this experience has helped me to evolve, but it has taken me a very long time to come to that conclusion. Being violated left me unable to trust those closest to me and I was also unable to allow myself to be touched or hugged. It was a long-term stressor for me, as I had to tear down my internal walls. I believe this also put a wedge between my mother and I as I felt that she was not there to protect or defend me during that time. This experience had made me more aware, as my children grew into adolescents, as to what they may encounter in life, therefore I had always kept a close watch and an open mind regarding the topic of sex.

My parents' constant arguing and fighting was a long-time stressor for us all. I believe that time had its effects on each one of us in different ways leading to our own personal behaviors. Anxiety and Over-Compulsive Disorder (OCD) are two disorders that come to mind, as a result of living in a hostile environment for so many years. My parents divorced after thirty-seven years of marriage. As I grew into a woman and later on had my own marital problems, it was then that I was able to relate to my mom. She had low self-esteem and no confidence because of the way my dad treated her. I found myself in a similar situation later on in my own marriage.

In my late twenties I began to suffer from frequent migraine headaches and did not know why. I was examined by a neurologist during that time and I was asked if I had a lot stress in my life. I never heard the word before, nor did I think my life was stressful. I thought this was the way life should be while raising a young family. My late husband and I suffered with great financial difficulty causing a lot of stress and tension. Our once loving environment in which we lived had become hostile. This lasted for approximately ten years leaving me with low self-esteem and no confidence whatsoever. I felt so low and depressed, and it showed. After twenty-four years of marriage I had become an empty shell.

During that same time, my father-in-law was diagnosed with congestive heart failure. He was constantly in and out of the hospital. He had open heart surgery which basically bought him five more years of life. Life became even more stressful, as it was difficult to make any plans as we were constantly running to the hospital to visit him. Our lives were on hold for thirteen years. When he passed away in 1999, it was somewhat of a relief not to see him suffer or struggle to live anymore. It was a very long and stressful time for us all.

Two weeks after the passing of my father-in-law, my family and I moved from Staten Island to Queens. During that time my family and I suffered from depression. We had moved and my husband and I were both unemployed for a short time until our lives picked up once again. The stress levels were high in my home. It was an extremely tense time.

My only compensation during that time was the fact that my dad lived nearby and I would see him more often. It was short-lived, as I lost my dad suddenly and tragically when he suffered a massive heart attack while he was arguing with my late husband, as I had mentioned earlier. He died in my home in front of my children and I. It was devastating to stand by and watch as my dad took his last breath. I remember feeling helpless as I waited for the paramedics to arrive. Minutes seemed like hours as I regressed into a very young child, as I kept saying to him, "Daddy, please don't leave me." My dad's death was a turning point for me in my life. I lost my best friend and sense of security. He was always there for me when life became too difficult. It was now time for me to grow up. It was during that time when I came to realize that my dad was an enabler to me. Helping and enabling are two very different things. Within two years, I had lost my two dads, whom I loved and enjoyed dearly. I cherish the years I had with them and I am grateful for the times we shared. That was when my healing journey began. My journey went as far back as childhood. I learned so much from that point on. I had read many self-help books to help me cope and understand.

Three years later, my husband was killed by a drunk driver. This sudden and tragic experience will stay with my family and I for the rest of our lives. I had to learn how to live with it. When you first hear the news, you are in a state of shock. The depression and devastation was unbearable. My children and I have had the unpleasant experience of visiting the morgue and seeing my husband's lifeless body, as his brains were splattered outside of his skull. We stood by and watched as he was buried and laid to rest. Still, after knowing all of this, it still seemed so surreal. I do, however, remember feeling a sense of relief, as all of the tension that he had caused had now disappeared. At that time, I would not think of sharing my thoughts with anyone as it would seem insensitive, harsh and cold. I do know I was not the only one who felt that way. There was a certain amount of guilt that accompanied that feeling, which was another emotion I had to deal with.

Soon after my late husband's death, I noticed a sense of distance or disassociation among my children, as they were all in a state of denial or in a total state of shock because of what had happened. It was a very lonely time, as we all had a different type of relationship with my husband. I can remember soon after the crash, I would have reoccurring nightmares of seeing or reenacting the crash. After the funeral, the vision of my husband's lifeless body at the morgue or in his casket would haunt me - it was difficult to close my eyes at night and try not to envision that. There was a lot of emotional numbness, especially during the first year. The anxiety, depression and devastation that I felt was unbearable. My children were afraid every time I left the house with the fear of me never returning. There was definitely increased anxiety, as mentioned in the referenced article, and concentration was extremely difficult during that time. Everyone was very irritable. It was extremely difficult to function on a daily basis, I slept a lot. It was a huge effort just trying to get up out of bed to face another day. My two youngest children and I acted out with self-destructive behaviors for a short period of time.

My son was acting out by driving recklessly, staying out late, not communicating and eventually dropping out of school. I had to let go of that "I feel sorry for him" mode. He took total advantage of the fact that his father was gone and no longer had to answer to him. Eventually, I took his car away, so that he would not harm himself or anyone else.

I speak to him more now without reprimanding and judging
him. He found his therapy through music, he writes the
lyrics and composes the music. You can feel and hear his
pain in his songs. He also found comfort in listening
to his father's music. My son is also an amazing poet. He
returned to school for a brief time and dropped out again.
Five years later, my son moved into his own apartment.
This was a very melancholy time and another type of loss. I
remember feeling proud as I felt a sense of accomplishment,
that my son was ready to live on his own, yet I feared for his
safety and well-being. Prior to his moving out, I had let go
of my resentment towards him. I became resentful as he did
not contribute financially or physically to our household. He
did not appreciate inheriting the role of the "man of the
house" at such a young age. He left on good terms, as he

needed his freedom in order to grow and evolve. He is a very deep and philosophical person and he continues to work through his own issues through his life's journey. There are certain times when a young man needs his father, it is during those times that my heart aches for him.

My youngest daughter has finally become more vocal about the whole experience. In the past, she would avoid telling people or would try to hide the fact that her father was dead whenever she was asked about him. It was just too painful for her to talk about. Her high school years were a blur as she was in denial and depression. I would explain to her that this was not something to be ashamed of and that she should talk about it more. Most of her life she has been surrounded by loss and death of some kind, her grandfathers and then her father. She is now learning to face her fears as she grows older. We never mourned together as a family, we went our separate ways to mend.

The second year following this tragedy was so much more profound. Reality had set in and the numbness was starting to dissipate. We were all still in such a bad place. I can remember feeling like I was at the bottom of a deep, dark well and there was nobody there to pull me out. It was an extremely lonely time for me. When I crawled out of that dark place, I emerged as a completely different person. I was vulnerable and I was acting so out of character. I was so angry and grief stricken. I felt that it did not pay to be good, so I was going out and behaving very badly, not caring about anyone or anything. My anger and frustration led to my own self-destructive behavior. It led me to lustful acts and gluttony. I had become a rebellious teenager all over again. I was with my late husband since I was seventeen years old. I regressed back to my teenage years and started to go out to the bars in the old neighborhood, expecting everything to be exactly the same as it was thirty years prior. This was not so. I did not know anyone at these places and I was now old enough to be their mother. During that very vulnerable time, I had met a man who really made me feel good again. He made me feel desirable and wanted again. I had not felt that way for a very long time. It was scary at first, but then it became very exciting. There were no ties or commitments. He was somewhat of a comfort to me, but later I realized he was a person I should not have been with. After a few months of this insanity, I woke up one morning and thought to myself, "What am I doing? Who am I?" I felt as if a stranger had taken over my body, this was not me. I always had good morals. How could I have done something so horrible? My sexual promiscuity was a direct result of post-traumatic stress. This was my destructive behavior. That time ended and I woke up. I have learned that I would and could not ever judge another person for their actions, no matter how severe they are. I would not have wanted anyone to pass judgment on me during that time. You never know what might be going on in someone's mind or in their life to make them behave so strangely. I have learned that grief is an emotion that could easily be mistaken for other emotions, such as passion and lust. As I continued to date and go out, I had to learn all the rules of dating in today's society as it was so very different thirty years ago. My children and family were concerned with my strange behavior as I was not very discreet about my actions. My children began to lose respect for me and were truly beginning to hate me.

Later on, I had met a wonderful man, who I eventually married. He is kind, patient and understanding.

He truly is unique in the sense that we live with my late husband's ghost. My family members and friends have accepted him as my new companion. No one person can ever replace another. But we can have new additions in our lives. I can truly be myself now. We now share a very large and ever-growing blended family together. Accepting and respecting ourselves and our adult children as equals is the key to our happy family. It is wonderful to see and watch as we all continue to learn, grow and evolve together.

> *Love is the ability and willingness to allow*
> *those that you care for to be what they choose*
> *for themselves without any insistence that*
> *they satisfy you. (Wayne Dyer)*

Repairing One's Soul

I had once attended a lecture given on campus by Elie Wiesel, a Holocaust survivor and Nobel Prize Winner. As I listened to Mr. Elie Wiesel speak, I could not help but to reflect on my own personal life experiences. He spoke of repairing the world, humanity and our souls. He spoke of the effect of death and survival. He also spoke of morality, loyalty and indifference.

Elie mentioned how the unthinkable can happen and the impossible can become possible. I know that all too well as I recalled the deaths of my dad and my husband. Each one had died suddenly and tragically. I can remember feeling devastated, angry, anxious, afraid and depressed. The death of my father was my turning point and the death of my husband was my awakening.

Elie also spoke of the art of survival. He spoke of
what was necessary in order to survive - such as generosity,
hope, solidarity and the passion for learning. I have
experienced it all. It is the reason for my well-being. The
generosity that was given to me during those extremely
difficult times in my life was overwhelming. It left me
feeling hopeful. I was also fortunate to have had an
enormous amount of support from family and friends. I
knew that I needed to learn in order to understand. After my
father's death, a very dear friend sent me several books to
read. That was when I began to learn. I continued to learn
so much about life through education. I realize that
everything truly is inter-relational. I have also met the most
amazing people during my training to become a victim
advocate for the Mothers Against Drunk Driving

organization. I have met people with the saddest stories, I remember looking at them and thinking, "How could you be so happy?" I now understand how and why.

Elie also spoke of how death can hold you as a prisoner. I could not agree more. I can remember feeling imprisoned in that very dark place. Once I emerged from the darkness, I began to live again. It is a slow process, it has been several years since my healing journey began and it still continues. I think life in general is a work in progress. There is always room for self-improvement. I chose living over dying. Life truly is so worth living. I am seeing the world for the very first time, at least that is how I perceive it. As for death, it is part of life. It is the end of one journey, but the beginning of a new journey. I have learned to accept death in a better light and I now I see it is a celebration.

Elie also spoke of loyalty to those we have lost. He stated that loyalty should not take place at the cost of your own life and/or living. I have been there more times than I care to share. As for my dad, my loyalty will always be there, but in a good way, a happy way, like when I go fishing on Father's Day. I can feel him beside me as I fish on the boat we occasionally fished on. As for my husband, I remain loyal through my work with M.A.D.D., but I do not let it consume me. When I began speaking on the Victim Impact Panels, it was a place where I could go vent and talk about my experience. It was very therapeutic. As time moved forward, I had a new man in my life and when I spoke it began to pull me down as my emotions were out of control. I contemplated leaving the panel, as I did not want to keep reliving that time in my life. And then I realized, by speaking, I was raising awareness to help others. Through my training with M.A.D.D., I have met the most amazing people – psychologists and other victims and survivors. I have learned so much from these people. I wanted to get an idea of what my family was feeling or experiencing, so that I could better help them cope. I am a survivor, not a victim. I am now taking my tragedy and I am helping others. It is so fulfilling.

Elie spoke of ruins and rebuilding. I feel that life is a compilation of ruins. It is all about starting over and rebuilding your life at certain times. I have learned the most amazing things from the challenges that have crossed my path. I have learned how to rebuild on those ruins. Life is like a book filled with new chapters. Some chapters are better and some are worse.

Elie also spoke of learning for the soul and soul searching. When I returned to school several years ago, I was amazed at how I was able to relate to all my experiences from every class I have taken thus far. I now understand why some things had to happen. [Some things were unpleasant and harsh, as I came to realize why things were the way they were at times.] I have learned so many lessons and I have learned how damaging the acts of enabling and controlling can be. I have also learned that forgiveness is the key to happiness. Forgiving one's self is the hardest person to forgive. Though I listen so much more now, as my journey continues I have learned to put myself first. It's a good and healthy place to be. However, it is a very difficult task as a wife and mother, as family has always come first and I have been accustomed to being last on that list. I now enjoy every day of my life as if it were my last day, but also as if it were my first day. I see life through the eyes of a child.

The unthinkable can happen and will continue to happen. It is what life is all about, we can learn from it all. Change is good and confusion forces one to think. I continue to maintain a healthy balance. I take the time to live, laugh and love – even during a crisis. I no longer feel guilty when I choose not to be somewhere or do something. I have learned to step back at times.

I was impressed with Elie Wiesel, but unfortunately or fortunately, it all depends on how you perceive it, as something good can come from something bad. I have learned life's lessons the hard way. All that he spoke of, I can relate to. I am more humble and compassionate because of it all. I am a better person today because of all that I have endured. Out of despair come the greatest gifts. I have learned to strategize, not agonize, over things that happen in life. I continue to have a passion for learning, as it has helped repair my soul. With all my new found knowledge I can now rebuild on those ruins.

> *There is divine beauty in learning... To learn means to accept the postulate that life did not begin at my birth. Others have been here before me, and I walk in their footsteps. The books I have read were composed by generations of fathers and sons, mothers and daughters, teachers and disciples. I am the sum total of their experiences, their quests. And so are you. (Elie Wiesel)*

Current Issues

I became a wife, a stepmother and a grandmother within four days. I had so much to look forward to. It was a new beginning for us all. I was also a college student working towards my Bachelor's degree. I became a psychology major and a philosophy minor to learn more about myself and those closest to me. I enjoyed school during this stage of my life. School had been extremely therapeutic for me. It is my enlightenment.

As mentioned earlier, I am also a speaker for MADD. I continue to speak twice a month to drunk drivers who are on probation. I occasionally speak to college students to help raise awareness. When I speak, I recall all my husband's finest qualities. As mentioned earlier, my children and I did eventually meet with the drunk driver who killed my husband. It went as well as could be expected. We talked and we cried. We have all forgiven him and departed on good terms. I had forgiven him many years ago, but I did not have the chance to verbalize it to him until that day we met.

I had recently lost my mother, as dementia had claimed her life. I feel as if I lost her many years ago, perhaps I never really had her. It was extremely difficult to watch her slow demise. I feel relieved that she is now gone, as we all suffered with her. It was a very long goodbye. It was not until after her death and as my daughter's wedding day was approaching that I began to write…poems especially, just like my mom. I had never written before and now I cannot stop.

Within one year my oldest daughter got married and she had her first baby. Four days before the birth of my first grandchild, I was married for the second time. My late husband continues to be very missed on every special occasion and for every milestone. However, I continue to stay in the moment and make new memories with my new husband and family.

Within our first year of marriage, it was a bit overwhelming as our new large family became a reality. Our adult children continue to figure out their lives and their futures, as our grandson is experiencing things in life for the very first time. My husband and I feel like spectators as we stand by and watch them all grow and mature. As a parent and grandparent, there is no greater joy! Spending time with my grandson reminds me of my past and my future. There

are times when he resembles my daughter so much that

its mind blowing, as it takes me back to another place and

time. When my grandson sees me, he greets me with the

biggest smile and he gets so excited...it is priceless! I now

understand why my mom was so crazy in love with her

grandchildren, they were the only happiness she had in her

life. I cherish my alone time with my grandson and hope to

be a better and more educated grandmother than I was as a

young mother.

As I sat with my academic advisor for one last time

before graduation, I took a good long look at all the classes I

had taken. The feeling was pride and yet I still felt some

disbelief in thinking that the student's name on the paper was

my own. I was inducted into two honor societies - The

Psi Chi Psychology International Honor Society and the Phi Sigma Tau International Honor Society and I managed to maintain a high GPA throughout my school years. I did not know what to think about my inductions, until I sat there and listened to the speakers, I then realized that this was quite an accomplishment. All my hard work had definitely paid off and never did I think I would be in any honor society whatsoever. I felt as if there was a light at the end of the tunnel, almost feeling as if I was climbing out of Plato's cave. It has taken me nine years to get here, intellectually and philosophically. I thoroughly enjoyed all of it and I find myself wanting to continue on to a Master's degree. School has become a crucial part in my healing journey. Looking over the last nine years of my life, I feel metamorphasized and enlightened!

Conclusion

I had declared psychology as my major and philosophy as my minor. I realize that they are inter-related subjects and overlap in some areas. Psychology is all about how the brain works and why people behave the way that they do. Whereas, philosophy is all about a person's thoughts and beliefs about living a good life. If one has good thoughts, one will behave properly, for the most part. If one can live free of ill thoughts and concepts, he or she will mentally and physically be well and brain healthy. A person's psychological health affects his or her mental state and well-being. And learned behavior and genetics can play a role in both psychology and philosophy. This would explain why I have spent the last several years of my life erasing what I was taught by my uneducated parents; such as martyrdom, the unequal roles of spouses and parents, disrespect for one another, passing judgment, constant yelling with no one listening or hearing what the other is saying and the lack of sex education. I do not recall seeing my parents show any signs of affection whatsoever, there was no communication or touching, yet I know that they cared for one another. Never did I see them hold hands or walk arm-in-arm.

> *Because we have grown up with our parents, we don't always recognize if their patterns of communication are unhealthy. For us, it is simply the way it has always been. It often takes someone outside the family to help us understand why the patterns need to be changed. (Gary Chapman)*

I now enjoy the sense of touch and I hug my husband and children every chance I get. I even embrace strangers! I now consider myself as an equal to my husband and adult children, I am not their superior or matriarch. I do not sit around waiting for my children to call or visit, simply because I am their mother. If I want to speak to them, I will call them. I live with no expectations on a daily basis or during special occasions and holidays. I make no demands on my husband or on my children, if they want to come visit or call, I would rather they did it in their own time and at their own convenience, simply because they want to. In today's society it is all about scheduling time and planning ahead due to different work schedules. I truly appreciate and accept my family and friends as they are. I have learned that silence is golden and I do my best to stay quiet unless I am asked for advice. As for sex, we speak openly and freely about the topic and my children know they can come to me regarding any sexual situation they encounter.

I do believe that writing helps improve your mental health. Facebook has become a sounding board, where you can see people venting on a daily basis.

> The original theory that motivated the first studies on writing was based on the assumption that not talking about important psychological phenomena is a form of inhibition. Whereas, inhibition appears to contribute to long-term health problems and the evidence that disclosure reduces inhibition and thereby improves health.
>
> (Pennebaker, p. 164)

As I sit at my computer, I continue to type. My thoughts just flow out from my fingertips. It is much easier typing my words, than having to speak them. I think nothing of sitting down and writing someone a letter, letting them know how I feel towards them. I simply enjoy putting my thoughts and feelings on paper...good, bad and indifferent.

The use of a computer makes it easier to write and you always have access to continue to add to your memoir as I have. I believe that you are less inhibited when writing than when speaking to someone, as you can be totally honest with yourself and not be concerned about being judged. I have found that writing has become very therapeutic. I no longer have any inhibitions, my life is an open book. That is something my children at times do not appreciate. I am too honest and upfront with them to the point where they think I am being rude or raunchy because I say it like it is. However, it saddens me to see how many unhappy young people there are out there online, who struggle with simple everyday stuff.

The events that have occurred over my lifetime have led to my current state of mind. I now feel compassion for those who struggle. Many tragic events have occurred, which has led to my self-examination. Life is **L**essons **I**ntended **F**or **E**volving. It continues as long as I am still alive and breathing. There is a message to be found in every mess of our lives. Coincidently, the word **mess** lies within the word **mess**age. I have found that I learn something new every day. And I now welcome change and embrace all that is summoned to me. I have had many turning points and awakenings before I was able to reach my inner peace and true happiness. I have learned how to be in total control of my thoughts and how to remain in a peaceful, happy state most of the time. I am amazed by all that I have learned thus far. I am thankful for all my heartaches and grateful for new beginnings. It is never too late to learn.

I have learned to control what and how I think. As my fiftieth birthday and Mother's Day were approaching, my son wrote the most amazing letter to me. I will share part of his letter. He wrote:

> *You and I make an awesome team. We are watching each other grow. You have been suppressed for the longest time...doesn't matter by what or whom. You have just been a sleeping giant and it is incredible to realize that at fifty. Your thoughts, ideas, and most*

importantly your morals…you are like someone so different. You basically turned twenty or thirty, but you know that better than I do. You have a whole new life ahead of you with everything you are doing. Fate is just nuts and crazy, but there are just things about dad's death that never ends…I feel like he was some kind of martyr for breaking us all out. Something about his death made us who we are all supposed to be. Ma, try to live a montage in your mind about where you came from and all the stuff in between, and how you are now. The feeling you get when you are done is so powerful. Man, sometimes I feel we are one of the strongest families that ever

lived. Ma, greatness to you! You did real
well and you are only doing better. Dignitally
signed, your fan, your son, Pete.
(Pete Romano)

This is my montage! And it is a great feeling to write it all down and revisit it from time to time. It has been a very long journey, a long and winding road. I am grateful for the life I have lived up to now. I could not have asked my son for a better gift – his words, his feelings and his support. He really touched me and made me realize that we are all evolving together. We are all branching out in our own lives, separately and on our own. My son has realized so much at such a young age. He is ready to begin his own montage! He understands so much more now.

The following is another note he sent me:

> *I need you for a lot of things, Ma. But I need*
>
> *you most as my last resort judge and my most*
>
> *precious audience... and you've been perfect. I*
>
> *love you unconditionally, and you've made me*
>
> *so proud in the last couple of years, to see*
>
> *how full of life and to see all your potential*
>
> *that you've been harboring your ENTIRE life*
>
> *finally come to fruition before it's too late...*
>
> *because you're actually happy now.*
>
> *(Pete Romano)*

Happiness comes from within, however it cannot be achieved unless all the anger and bitterness is released and let go. It takes many years to change your thoughts and behavior and it is a very difficult task for most people, myself included. In my last philosophy class, on the last day of the semester, my professor stated a quote by Tom Robbins, "It's never too late to have a happy childhood." Now that I have worked through all of my issues of the past, and I can truly understand all that has happened, I have eliminated all that pain and anger of yesteryear from within. I can honestly say that my childhood may not have been so bad…it was just life. As life continues to move forward, I will continue to learn how to be a stepmother and a grandmother. I have learned to embrace and enjoy my family like never before. It has been somewhat overwhelming, but in a good way.

For most of my life I have been misunderstood, misread and misjudged. My reasons for writing this book are to help others understand one another, as one never truly knows what is going on in one's life or mind. I no longer wait until someone is dead before I try to understand them, as I did not truly understand my parents and my husband until they were gone. So much patience and tolerance are needed in order to do so. I now have a much deeper appreciation for them.

Passing judgment on others is something I would advise against and suggest never judging another person by their actions or non-actions, as one never know what it's like to walk in their shoes. That old saying, "Never judge a book by its cover", is so very true.

I want to make it a point that no one is exempt from a drunk driving crash, as it can happen to anyone. I lost two family members to a drunk driver on two separate occasions, decades apart. Prevention is the key, as M.A.D.D.'s mission continues to eliminate this serious problem.

And last but not least, my main purpose for sharing my story is to inspire others and help them understand that through reading, writing and learning one can overcome just about anything in life. It is possible to change your thoughts and your life, however one must invest the time to do so. My hope is to give others hope as it is never ever too late!

This book is a compilation of papers and speeches that I have made over the last decade of my life. I have been encouraged by my professors and my son to share my story and it was with great hesitation that I put it all together. I now embrace my pain and anger, although it will always reside within me. I have no malice here, but I am aware there may be some repercussions once this book is published as with any work that goes public. My only purpose is to reach out to others to let them know that they are not alone. My perception of the truth may vary from other family members and friends, as my journey and personal truth are my own.

For those who are stuck in the darkness of the cave, there are free programs out there to help aid and guide you through the most difficult of times, through communities, churches, schools or non-profit organizations. Do not be ashamed or embarrassed if medication and psychological therapy are needed to help you achieve your state of well-being. Face your fears. The first step is to become aware of your thoughts and behavior, only then will your healing journey begin. The journey will not be an easy one, as you will need to revisit the pain that dwells inside you.

I am not looking for sympathy for my sorrows or accolades for my accomplishments. I have met the most amazing people with the most heroic stories and outcomes along my path. There are no comparisons here, some stories are much worse and some are much better. By hearing and sharing our stories we learn and grow together…it is that simple. I have also accepted the fact that not everyone will like me and some may be offended by what I do, say or write. My mind is clear and I am at peace. My enlightenment has led me to freedom. I had come across the following quote and it hangs near my desk:

> *What is life for? It is for you. The best day of your life is the one on which you decide is your own. No apologies or excuses. No one to lean on, rely on, or blame. The gift of life is yours – it is an amazing journey – and you alone are responsible for the quality of it. This is the day your life really begins.*
>
> *(Abraham Maslow)*

I now choose to live by these words. I am a survivor and no longer a victim. In this last decade I have been asked by so many people, "How did you do it? How did you get here?" There is not just one simple answer, as it is different for each individual. For me it was the passion for learning, along with all the generosity, encouragement and love I felt from others. My hope is to raise awareness in others in order to help them become hopeful and encouraged as I have been from all I have read. I had read and listened to works by Wayne Dyer, Eckhart Tolle, Gary Chapman, Josh Olsteen and Maya Angelou, to name a few, who have all had their share of pain, sorrow and loss. I am so thankful to them for sharing their stories. I am thankful for all the people who have come in and out of my life over this past decade. There are a handful of people in my life who have truly been there and continue to be there for my children and I, for whom I will always be extremely thankful for. As the tenth anniversary of my late husband's death approaches, I reflect on all the trials and tribulations that my family and I have experienced along the way. One has a choice to succumb or overcome, both roads will decide who or what one becomes. I am ever so grateful for the past, the present and the future. However, I am staying in the present and I am appreciating each day I am given…one day and one moment at a time. Here is another song that really sums up life itself and overcoming life's difficulties. It is a journey that so many people can relate to. I love this song!

Life is Sweet

by Natalie Merchant

It's a pity, it's a crying shame

He pulled you down again

How painful it must be

To bruise so easily inside

It's a pity, it's a downright crime

It happens all the time

You want to stay your little daddy's girl

You want to hide from a vicious world outside

Don't cry

You know the tears will do no good, so dry your eyes

Oh, your daddy, he's the iron man

Battleship wrecked on dry land

Your mama, she's a bitter bride, she'll never be satisfied

Do you know? And that's not right

But don't cry

You know the tears will do no good, so dry your eyes

Oh, they told you life is hard, misery from the start

It's dull, it's slow, it's painful

But, I'll tell you life is sweet inspite of the misery

There's so much more to be grateful

Well, who do you believe?

Who will you listen to? Who will it be?

'Cause it's high time that you decide

In your own mind

I've tried to comfort you

I've tried to tell you to be patient

They are blind

And they can't see

Fortune gonna come one day, all gonna fade away

Your daddy, the war machine

And your momma, the long and suffering

Prisioner of what she cannot see

For they told you life is hard, misery from the start

It's dull, it's slow, it's painful

But, I'll tell you life is sweet inspite of the misery

There's so much more, be grateful

So, who will you believe?

Who will you believe? Who will it be?

Because it's high time that you decide

It's time to make up your own, your own state of mind

Oh, they told you that life is long, be thankful when it's done

Don't ask for more, be grateful

But, I'll tell you life is short be thankful

Because before you know it will be over

'Cause life is sweet

Life is, oh, so very short, life is sweet

And life is, oh, so very short

Life is sweet

With the help of philosophy, I have weeded through the weeds or koans of my life, helping me to see clearly.

Koans are records of how particular masters tried to help students "let go" of certain ignorant attachments, how they tried to awaken them to a certain aspect of reality.

But actually such awakening is not a matter

of finding the one fixed "right way" to look at

things. The point is to be free of all fixed,

locked-in, dogmatic perspectives, and to

adopt, spontaneously and compassionately,

whatever approach helps others to get

unstuck from their attachments. When we

begin, we think that good and bad, you and

me, high and low, buddha and non-buddha,

etc. are really different, so we have to unlearn

this. But if we think that means that these

things really are the same, then we have still

more unlearning to do. A famous Ch'an

saying: Shakyamuni Buddha is still sitting.

(http://www.chsbs.cmich.edu/guy_newland/re

l_320/handouts/zen/koan-philosophy.htm)

As my life continues to move forward I still have so much more to learn and unlearn. After fifty plus years, mourning has broken and I have finally come out of the dark…my darkness!

For in the end, it is all about memory, its

sources and its magnitude, and, of course, its

consequences. (Elie Wiesel)

"All of these lines across my face
Tell you the story of who I am
So many stories of where I've been
And how I got to where I am
But these stories don't mean anything
When you've got no one to tell them to
It's true..." (Brandi Carlile)

"...The laughter and the tears

The shadows of misty yesteryears

The good times and the bad you've seen

And all the others in between

Remember, do you remember

The times of your life (do you remember)

Reach back for the joy and the sorrow

Put them away in your mind

The mem'ries are time that you borrow

To spend when you get to tomorrow..."

("Times of Your Life" by Paul Anka)

❖

"...I couldn't see it

Until I let go

Gave into love and watched all the bitterness burn

Now I'm coming alive

Body and soul

And feelin' my world start to turn

And I'll taste every moment

And live it out loud

I know this is the time,

This is the time

To be more than a name

Or a face in the crowd

124

I know this is the time

This is the time of my life

Time of my life…

But now I'm rising from the ashes

Finding my wings

And all that I needed

Was there all along

Within my reach

As close as the beat of my heart"

("The Time of My Life" by David Cook)

❖

"…And in the end, the love you take is equal to the love you make…" *("The End" by The Beatles)*

References

Elias, Marilyn. "You've Got Trauma, But Writing Can
  Help". USA Today, 2008.

Koan-Philosophy.
<http://www.chsbs.cmich.edu/guy_newland/rel_320/handout
s/zen/koan-philosophy.htm>.

Mitchell, Stephen. <u>The Tao te Ching</u>, Harper Collins, 2006.

Pennebaker, James W. "Writing About Emotional
  Experiences as a Therapeutic Process".
  Psychological Science, Vol. 8, No. 3. May 1997.

"Post-traumatic Stress Disorder (PTSD): Symptoms, Types
and Treatment". 28 Sept. 2007.
<www.helpguide.org.>

Ryckman, Richard M. Theories of Personality. Wadsworth
Cengage Learning, 2008.

Wiesel, Eli. "Repairing the World" (Lecture), Long Island
University, C.W. Post Campus, 2008.

www.ingramcontent.com/pod-product-compliance
Lightning Source LLC
Chambersburg PA
CBHW030502100426

42813CB00002B/309